PUBLISHING

OMF International works in most East Asian countries, and among East Asian peoples around the world. It was founded by James Hudson Taylor in 1865 as the China Inland Mission. Our overall purpose is to glorify God through the urgent evangelisation of East Asia's billions, and this is reflected in our publishing.

Through our books, booklets, website and quarterly magazine, *East Asia's Billions*, OMF Publishing aims to motivate Christians for world mission, and to equip them for playing a part in it. Publications include:

- contemporary mission issues
- the biblical basis of mission
- the life of faith
- stories and biographies related to God's work in East Asia
- accounts of the growth and development of the church in Asia
- studies of Asian cultures and religion relating to the spiritual needs of her peoples

Visit our website at *www.omf.org*

Addresses for OMF English-speaking centres can be found at the back of this book.

[prayer > in Hard Places

j a n g r e e n o u g h

MONARCH
B O O K S
Mill Hill, London & Grand Rapids, Michigan

First published by Monarch Books in 2002,
Concorde House, Grenville Place,
Mill Hill, London NW7 3SA.

Published in conjunction with OMF.

Distributed by:
UK: STL, PO Box 300, Kingstown Broadway, Carlisle,
Cumbria CA3 0QS;
USA: Kregel Publications, PO Box 2607,
Grand Rapids, Michigan 49501.

ISBN 1 85424 583 X

British Library Cataloguing Data
A catalogue record for this book is available
from the British Library

Book design and production for the publishers by
Gazelle Creative Productions Ltd,
Concorde House, Grenville Place, Mill Hill, London NW7 3SA.

Contents

Acknowledgements

Eileen Crossman, *Mountain Rain*, OMF 1982.
Catherine L. Davis, *The Spirits of Mindoro*, OMF/
   Monarch Books 1998.

Elder Brother
Number Three

In 1979 a curious document arrived in England. It was a certificate of honour, written in the language of the Lisu people of China, and it was addressed to a man who had been dead for forty years.

> From the time of the establishment of the Lisu church in the Shan States, Kokong County, Six Families District, Muddy Pool Village in 1920 until 23rd December 1978 there are 58 years. Within that period, Rev. J. O. Fraser, Elder Brother Number Three, since you served willingly and warmheartedly, doing the work of the church of Jesus Christ in obedience to the command of God, the leaders of the church present you with this certificate of honour.
>
> *Date:* 1978, 12th month, 26th day
> *Place:* Lashio, New Village, Burma

The Lisu church had been through difficult times since its founding in 1920: overrun by the

Japanese invasion in 1942, persecuted by the Chinese Communist government in 1949, and deprived of any overseas support when the missionaries were forced to leave the country in 1951. Many Lisu moved across the border into Burma in these years, continuing to lead and teach their own churches even after all the missionaries were expelled from Burma in 1963. By the end of the 1960s they were helped by the arrival of the complete Bible in their own language, the fruit of many years' faithful work by those exiled missionaries and their helpers.

In 1978 the leaders of the Lisu church in Burma decided to celebrate the founding of their local church, some ten years before; they also wanted to celebrate the founding of their parent church in Lisuland in 1920. They sent a certificate of honour to Allyn Cooke, an American who had worked in the area for many years – and also, posthumously, to the man who had first walked the hills of China seeking out the Lisu tribal people, learning their language and living their life, and bringing them the news of the gospel.

From those few peasants who accepted Christ into their lives in the primitive villages of southwest China, a great church has grown up. By the 1990s there were about 200,000 Lisu Christians – around 35 per cent of the total Lisu population of 575,000. In Fugong County in China, nearly 66 per cent of the population was Christian, rising to 98 per cent in certain villages. The Chinese government was considering declaring them officially a Christian minority in the whole of China. The extraordinary growth of this Christian community has been due to the efforts of many people, some of whose names will never be known. But the Lisu church has not forgotten James Fraser, the man they knew as Mr Fu, or Elder Brother Number Three.

The paths of life

James Outram Fraser was born in 1886, the third son of a successful veterinary surgeon who practised in St Albans. His parents separated when he was in his teens, and his mother took all five children to live with her in Letchworth. James was a brilliant scholar and musician: he gave his first public piano recital at the age of 20, when he was studying engineering at Imperial College, London. He was an energetic, popular young man, with a tremendous sense of humour and a ringing laugh, who loved company, strenuous exercise and mountaineering. He clearly had a brilliant career ahead of him in a field where there was considerable wealth to be made: Great Britain was still an imperial power, and her engineers were in demand all over the world. His prospects were excellent, and his path seemed to be mapped out.

That path was changed by a leaflet given to him by a fellow student, which spoke of God's plans for the individual – better plans and better prospects than the world could offer. It pointed out that millions of people had never heard of Jesus Christ, in spite of the Great Commission which he had given his followers: "Go and make disciples of all nations." Like the rest of his family, James had been brought up as a Methodist, and had taken his faith seriously. But now, like John Wesley, he found his heart "strangely warmed", and began to follow his master in a new way, reading his Bible, studying and praying with the disciplined concentration and perseverance that characterised so much of what he did.

During those days, as he studied for his degree, James also went to hear the great preachers of the day. That was how he came to meet C. T. Studd at a Christian training camp in 1906, and how he first learned about the China Inland Mission, founded by Hudson Taylor to take the gospel into that vast and largely unknown country. James liked what he heard about the mission: the fact that it was interdenominational, basing its faith upon the Bible but taking little note of minor doctrinal differences between churches; and the fact that it made no appeals for money, but lived by faith in God's provision – a provision which enabled it to support over a thousand members. So it was to CIM that he applied as soon as he had completed his degree.

He met with some opposition from his family (who had doubts about "this peculiar bunch" of missionaries who were not formally attached to any church) and from the mission itself, which initially rejected him on health grounds because he had a minor ear infection. James did not give up, however, and at the age of twenty-one he was accepted for the year-long training in North London. By the time he was twenty-two he was already riding on horseback across the mountain ranges of south-west China.

Faithful in small things

To a man who had enjoyed climbing and walking holidays in the Alps, travel in Yunnan province was exhilarating. "This lofty, scrubby, rocky, wet, wild country – how I just revel in it!" he wrote. "Wet, silent, lonely – not even the call of a bird – it must have been some 10,000 feet high, and most of the year covered with snow."

Nevertheless, once he was settled in his first home, a small, bare, rat-infested room above a Chinese inn, he was assailed by loneliness. There were no Europeans in the small town of Tengyueh other than his fellow workers, Mr and Mrs Embery, who were busy with their own work, and James knew that before he could begin on his own he had to develop some degree of fluency in Chinese. His six months of language study were only a small beginning. So he embarked on a programme of Bible study, prayer, language study and practice, and, after a while, his first attempts at preaching. It was frustrating, when his work depended so much on imparting the word of God, to be unable to find the right words in the new language; as a result, James schooled himself to work hard at mastering the seemingly trivial tasks of vocabulary and intonation. Hudson Taylor said, "A little thing is a little thing. But faithfulness in a little thing is a great thing." It was in this spirit that James approached every aspect of his new life in China.

When he travelled to other towns, he travelled light, carrying only a change of clothes, a blanket and a few small books and tracts. One American missionary reported meeting him on a mountain road: the American had coolies and a mule carrying his luggage, camp bed and cooking equipment. "In the middle of nowhere, I met James ambling along with a small bag on his back, free as air and happy as a sandboy. I took him for a Chinese coolie at first."

He was also faithful to the rules of the missionary society, which forbade any requests for donations. When he was forced to stay in Burma to escape the bloodshed of the Republican Revolution in 1911, he found himself stranded without money or support. As the supplies in the mission home began to run out, he knew that he could not borrow money or run into debt, yet it seemed unlikely that his salary would reach him 1,600 miles from Shanghai, in a land torn by rebels and bandits. He prayed daily that God would remember his promises to supply our needs, and indeed on the very day when he had to pay his coolie, the money arrived in a registered letter. "It... has done not a little to strengthen my faith," he wrote to his mother. "The Lord, I believe, permitted the trial just to show me how he could deliver me out of it."

The Monkey People

Meanwhile, James was improving his language skills and preaching regularly in Tengyueh. It was here that he first saw the Lisu tribespeople, who came into the market to trade. They were a colourful sight: the women wore bright costumes, ornamented with shells and beads, and the men wore turbans, ornamental sashes, and white leggings. The Chinese called them "Monkey People", because they lived high in the mountains. James tried to talk to them but found that their language differed from the Chinese he was learning, and they could not understand him. He knew that missionaries had been working among the tribes of eastern Yunnan, including the Miao and Lisu; now he was seized with a great desire to work with the western Lisu people. "I was very much led out in prayer for these people, right from the beginning. Something seemed to draw me to them," he said. Even so, he had been working in Tengyueh for almost a year before he was able to find a Lisu guide who would take him into the mountains.

The first trip was momentous: he was taken to a village called Pleasant Valley, where preparations were being made for a betrothal celebration. The village consisted of about twelve bamboo shacks inside a perimeter fence, and the people welcomed him cheerfully. They were a happy, hospitable group, and they gave him food and a place to sleep, in "a dirty old room in a Lisu house, everything smoked and black, huge grimy grain bins here and there, a dog or two running over the earthen floor." The celebrations next day included feasting on rice and goat's meat and a great deal of home-made wine. There was story-telling around a big log fire, and dancing which went on all night. The people were friendly and good-humoured, but after two days of drinking they were not in the mood to listen seriously to James's message. However, one man did ask him to visit his family at another village a few miles away.

James stayed for a week at the new village, some 7,000 feet up Trinket Mountain. Here, the people were willing to listen to him. He stayed with the Koh family, who, like all their neigh-bours, kept a demon shelf at the back of their house. This held a bowl of rice, an incense burner, and a bunch of leaves in which the spir-its were supposed to live. James did not know much about the tribal religion: the people believed that the spirit world was all around them, with powerful and unpredictable spirits living in rocks, trees and other places. Offerings and sacrifices had to be made to show gratitude to friendly spirits and to appease evil or troublesome ones, which might cause misfortune or death. It was a religion of fear.

Mr Koh and his four sons were interested in the story of the true God and his son Jesus Christ who loved people; they decided they wanted to please him, especially if he was stronger than all the other spirits. So they pulled down the demon shelf and put it on the fire in the middle of the room. James knew that the family understood very little of the gospel, but it was immensely encouraging to see such a result so quickly.

Not long afterwards James and Carl Gowman, an American missionary, were invited to another celebration, this time by the Tsai family, who lived in Six Family Hollow. Once again, there was much dancing and singing accompanied by great quantities of rice wine, but after the guests had left the family wanted to hear the gospel message. The Lisu loved music, and James was able to teach them some Chinese hymns and prayers. Even after the missionaries had left, they continued to hold evening prayers among themselves, with a special service on Sundays. They, too, destroyed their demon shelf and stopped making offerings to the spirits, and one of the Tsai family sons, called Old Five, accompanied James to other villages, translating and helping the people to pray in Lisu.

Roaming through the earth

However, this was not the breakthrough that James had hoped for. When he returned to visit the Koh family, he found that they had been under attack from the spirit world. The youngest son fell ill, and when their prayers failed to help him, the family made sacrifices to the spirits; he began to recover. Then, one evening, Koh Three had a violent outburst, which sounded as though he was possessed, and shortly afterwards the youngest brother relapsed and died. The wife of Koh Two committed suicide, and Koh Two ran away from the village. The family had been torn apart.

James was deeply concerned. It reminded him of the story in Luke 11:24–26, where a demon was cast out from a man and returned with seven more spirits. At first he found it hard to accept that demon possession could occur in the twentieth century as it had in the first, but he had no doubt that this was what had happened. It saddened him that the Lisu put all their troubles down to the fact that they had tried to become Christians, rather than to the fact that they had put themselves back into the spirits' power by reverting to worshipping the demons.

A similar fate awaited the Tsai family. A grandchild fell sick, and a local shaman told them that the spirits were taking revenge because they had pulled down their demon shelf. They erected a new shelf and promised to sacrifice a pig. Of the whole family, only Old Five held on to his new faith.

For the first time, James was forced to consider the true power that demon worship had over the Lisu people. The villagers were enslaved by their fear of the spirits. Sometimes the demon priests would appease the "great spirit" by getting people to walk up a ladder of sword blades – the victims would be "purified" and would climb the ladder naked and in a trance. They also heated chains in a fire and beat themselves with them, or walked on hot coals; at the same time they would sacrifice chickens to idols, by biting through their necks. James attended one of these festivals and observed that it was a ceremony of fear; the people did not view this as entertainment but as a terrifying ordeal.

It was clear to James that he had to take this religion seriously; so many of those who listened to his message at first would afterwards revert to the old ways as soon as some difficulty came along. Truly, Satan was "roaming through the earth and going to and fro in it".

The prayer of faith

The one crumb of comfort in these dark days was the arrival of a young man from the Karen tribe in Burma. Ba Thaw spoke both English and Lisu, he was well educated and a deeply spiritual Christian, and he was able to help both James and Old Five with their work. They continued to travel around the villages, telling the people that they could be free from fear, and that there was a

God who loved them and could bring them peace. At the same time James was conducting a simple survey of the area for the benefit of the mission. He concluded that in the northern area alone there were 300 towns and villages and around 10,000 Lisu, and even greater numbers of the Kachin tribe. Most of these people had never seen a European before.

The extent of the task was daunting. Apart from brief periods when he was accompanied by helpers from the mission, or by Old Five or Ba Thaw, James was working alone. The sheer physical challenge of travelling to the villages would have defeated a man with less stamina: the mountain ranges were desolate places, thousands of feet high. The settlements when he found them were primitive and dirty, and his bedding was usually infested with lice and bedbugs; in the winter and spring, the rain and mist seemed endless, and everything was permanently damp. The food was poor, and he was generally undernourished and a prey to illness; at various times he suffered repeated bouts of malaria, varicose ulcers on his legs and feet, pleurisy, bronchitis, and appendici-tis, which was successfully treated in Shanghai.

Although Tengyueh was still a base to which he could return, James now spent most of his time living in the mountains among the Lisu people. As he looked out from his leaky bamboo outhouse at the curtains of rain that shrouded the mountains, he grew increasingly depressed; he felt that a similar gloomy mist had settled on his spirit. He was full of doubt: his prayers went unanswered, the Lisu were not turning to Christ, and his whole life seemed pointless. Why had he given up his home comforts of body and mind – warm, clean, comfortable rooms; friends and family to love and talk and laugh with; the fellowship of other Christians in a church; the intellectual and artistic pursuits of work and music? He gave them up gladly when he believed that it was God who had called him to this life of austerity, but had he been deceiving himself? Perhaps there was no purpose in any of his activities. His despair was so deep that he longed for an ending – an accidental slip, perhaps, into a rocky ravine, or the river that roared in torrents down the mountainside.

Two things roused him from this terrible condition. The first was an article in a magazine called *The Overcomer*, sent to him from England. It showed him that "deliverance from the power of the Evil One comes through definite resistance on the ground of the Cross." It was one of those moments of insight which transform a life. "I felt like a man perishing from thirst, to whom some beautiful, clear cold water had begun to flow… the cloud of depression dispersed."

The other was the reassurance that he had the support of other Christians, who stood beside him in his battles, even though they were thousands of miles away. He had asked his mother to gather a group of like-minded friends to pray together for the work among the tribes. These faithful Christians made a commitment to pray for him regularly, and he responded by writing to them with vivid accounts of his activities in China. While these letters contained descriptions of people and landscapes which fascinated his prayer partners, they also shared the lessons that he was learning about prayer.

He felt that in the past, much of his prayer had been ineffective because it had lacked faith: he believed that God would answer his prayers one day, but not that they were already answered. Now he looked at things differently. "True faith glories in the present tense," he wrote. The full outworking of God's promises "is often in the future, but God's word is as good as his bond and we need have no anxiety." He also saw a distinction between "general" prayer and "definite" prayer. Where he knew little about a situation, he could only pray in generalities, though this was still a duty. But among the Lisu, in the matters close to his heart, he could pray specifically, where a "definite request was made in definite faith for a definite answer".

Now he felt that the time had come for him to make his own definite prayer of faith, and he recorded it in his diary: that God would bring several hundred Lisu families to saving faith in himself. He never prayed that prayer again, but trusted that he had already received the answer.

In the Lord's time

He was right, of course. One of the first believers who managed to keep the faith was Moh, a pastry-cook who lived at Hsiangta. James often stayed there on his travels, delighting in the fellowship he had with this bright, happy-go-lucky Christian who witnessed for Christ to the customers in his shop. It was Moh who made the first contact with the people of Cold Country, persuading them to invite a missionary to visit their villages and tell them about Jesus Christ. Yet Moh's own conversion had taken place long before.

On James's first solo journey out into the Chinese countryside he had taken with him some Christian literature, which he gave away free or sold for a few coins in the market-places. At a time when his own grasp of the language was still shaky, he felt it was important to leave something for the people to read after he had moved on. These colourful booklets proved popular: mostly they were translations of the Gospel of Mark, though they included some tracts and translations of sermons.

One day in the crowded market of Mangshih,

a town south of Paoshan, someone upset his little trestle table and all his booklets were thrown into the road. As James bent to gather them up and rescue what he could from the puddles, a six-year-old boy grabbed a Gospel and ran off with it, stuffing the bright red booklet down the front of his shirt as he ran. He knew that some of the books were given away free, so it was hardly stealing, and he knew his father would like to read it. The boy was the son of Moh, and he had come to Mangshih to sell some of his rich Chinese cakes. He carried the book home across the mountain trail to Hsiangta, where it began a work unaided by any missionary.

Five years later, James was travelling in the same area and visited Hsiangta for the first time. He preached in the market-place and at the end he asked if anyone wanted to know more about Jesus Christ, who was the Son of God. Moh Ting-Chang stepped forward; he said that he already believed that Jesus was the Son of God, and he wanted to follow him. He took James home to his little shop, and produced the well-thumbed copy of Mark's Gospel. He had read it many times, he said, since his little son had stolen it. He longed to know more about Jesus, because he was truly God come into the world.

Moh destroyed his demon shelf and committed himself to following Jesus, and became a brave and persistent witness for Christ. James had found him waiting for him, already a believer. God had prepared the first of his followers, long before James was ready to pray his prayer of faith.

The rising tide

James had been working and praying among the Lisu for over ten years, with very little response, other than the occasional encouragement like Ba Thaw and Moh. He said:

> I feel like a man who has his boat grounded in shallow water. Pull or push as he may, he will not be able to make his boat move more than a few inches. But let the tide come in and lift his boat off the bottom – then he will be able to move it as far as he pleases.

Now at last, after years of prayer, the spiritual tide was turning. Family after family came to James to say that they wanted to become Christians; they had heard his message on previous visits, and they had thought hard about it. They were ready to give up the old ways of spirit worship, and put their trust in the true God. They burned all the evidence of spirit worship and turned their lives around to follow Jesus. In the first village, seven families came together, so James was able to leave a little community to support each other as they grew in faith.

At Melting Pot village there were ten families; at Cypress Hill fifteen; at Turtle Village 24; at Mottled Hill 49. After only a few weeks, James found that 129 families had rejected the darkness of demon worship and turned to Christ, representing about 600 people. Suddenly, in answer to his prayer of faith, there was a young church growing among the Lisu people. When Ba Thaw arrived, James knew that he had found the perfect shepherd for the new flock: a native speaker who knew all the people and the villages and understood their way of life. Under his leadership, the church grew further and attracted yet more converts.

It was during this period that Moh persuaded

the Lisu of Cold County that James should visit them. He sent a postcard asking him to come, but it arrived while James was involved in organising the first Christian festival at Turtle Village; hundreds of people had travelled in across the mountains to share their faith and sing and pray together. James could hardly leave them. Instead, he sent a young American, Allyn Cooke, who had little knowledge of the Chinese language and no Lisu.

Allyn was willing to make the attempt, though he had little experience of the Lisu ways, and was puzzled by the fact that the interpreters and guides who travelled with him carried such large quantities of whisky. He managed to explain his message to the people, but the elders were unwilling to listen for long; they wanted to get on with the drinking. He sat in the headman's room and watched the dancing, drunkenness and debauchery that went on all night; he saw the tribespeople stagger in and bow down before the spirits of their ancestors. At last, he could control himself no longer and burst into tears.

Big Tiger, the headman, was astonished.

"What is wrong?" he asked. "I am weeping because you are lost without Jesus Christ," replied Allyn. Now he had their attention: they had never imagined that a white man could care about them so much. They listened to what he had to say, and the whole family decided to believe. Other villagers joined them, and Allyn went from house to house, giving his message and helping them to pull down their demon shelves. When he left, a few days later, the whole village and some nearby hamlets had turned to Christ.

After Allyn's departure, another message came from across the mountain: would someone come and tell the people there about Jesus? A Lisu boy was willing to go, and at least a hundred families there became Christians as a result.

James, meanwhile, had decided that the Lisu needed to be able to read the Gospels in their own language. This presented some difficulties, as the Lisu language differed from Chinese and had never been written down. With the help of Ba Thaw and some American missionaries in Burma, James devised a way of writing it, known as Fraser script; it resembled English capital letters, but with some letters reversed or upside down to represent sounds unique to the language. Then he translated Mark's Gospel and a catechism, and arranged to have them printed in Rangoon. Even before the printed books became available, he began to teach groups of people to read, using handwritten copies of the script. It was a vital step forward which gave the Lisu a new sense of identity: having even one book of the Bible available in their own language made it possible to spread the word more effectively.

Life in abundance

After years of working alone in the mountains, James married in October 1929. His wife was Roxie Dymond, the daughter of another missionary, Frank Dymond. Though she was nineteen years his junior, she was happy to join him in his austere life, travelling in the mountains and staying in poor Chinese inns. James felt that she was a better preacher than he was, and she always drew a crowd. Even after their two daughters were born, she continued to travel with him, though by now there were more helpers in the field, and other missionaries had come to share the burden of caring for the ever-increasing number of Christians in the area. They were able to share a permanent house with another missionary family, the Fitzwilliams, in a village near the Burmese border.

In 1934, they were able to visit friends and family in England and North America, returning to Shanghai in the spring of 1935. There, they were delayed for some months on mission business, though James was impatient to return to his work among the Lisu. Maud Taylor, of Auckland, New Zealand, paints a vivid picture of J. O. Fraser in those days. Maud is now 99 years old, but she remembers him clearly: she and her husband Harry were both CIM missionaries, in Shanghai for their wedding.

> He was a tall, well-framed, strong, healthy, athletic man, but not ungainly. He was a fine-looking man and had a nice voice and was quietly spoken. I think he was a gentleman in every sense of the word. He was not a bit austere or dominating at all. He was very normal, very gentle and warm-hearted. He

**was friendly, outgoing and pleasant to listen
to... He had a wife and two lovely children.
His wife was very clever, and the girls were
always beautifully dressed. He played the
piano for our wedding. We asked him if he
would do that, and he did it gladly. He was a
fine pianist.**

In 1938 Roxie was expecting their third child,
and the family went to stay in Paoshan. There,
James became ill and suffered from a severe
headache: it was cerebral malaria. Four days later,
he was dead. He was buried on a hill overlooking
Paoshan, in the mountains which had been his
home for thirty years.

Roxie was aware of God's protecting hand
over the rest of her family. She travelled to Burma
for the birth of her third daughter, and then went
on to Chefoo to take the other girls to the missionary school there. As a result, she was with her
girls at the time of the Japanese invasion, and was
evacuated with the school to the concentration
camp at Weihsien. It was a hard way to spend the
war years, but at least the little family were able
to be together, and to help each other through
their grief and the loss of a husband and father.

In another story, that would be the end – a man who lived and died. Other missionaries followed him and continued his work, and they too have died and gone to join him in glory. That is the difference for a Christian: this life is not all there is; death is not the end of the story, and heaven awaits us all. That is why so many have been and are still prepared to leave behind home, friends, familiar pleasures and comforts, and endure poverty and hardship to share the greatest gift of all – the gift of God's Son.

The message of the gospel is not just one of triumph over death, however. Jesus said, "I have come that they may have life, and have it to the full" (John 10:10). The daily walk with God is not just a promise of heaven in the future, but one of joy and fulfilment now. James Fraser's story is not only about courage and perseverance on the mission field, but about the growth of a great soul. He wrote home: "It seemed as if God was saying: 'You are crying to me to do a big work among the Lisu; I am wanting to do a big work in you yourself.' "

He learned about fellowship with God, and

the power of prayer. He spoke of the crucial breakthroughs in the work: the conversion of Moh, the day when Allyn Cooke wept for the spiritual darkness in the villages, and the willingness of the Lisu boy who crossed the mountains with the message. None of these events came about through James's own actions, but they were the fruits of his prayer and loving concern. This was the depth of his humility: he always knew that success rested on the grace of God and the work of the Holy Spirit.

As he went about his work and deepened his own spiritual life, he was teaching not only the Lisu, but also his prayer partners at home, through his letters and prayerful meditations. When Elder Brother Number Three went to his reward, he left a legacy not only to the Christians in China but to the Christian family all over the world, who benefited from the insights he gained as he went about his great work of prayer.

Finding the
Mission Field

Paul and Naomi Pruitt are missionaries. They have worked in Taiwan, China and Japan, and now once again they are living and working in a strange city, thousands of miles from home – Oxford, England. The story of their travels around the world shows how God can use people who are willing to trust him for the next step of their journey – even when it doesn't appear to be going in the direction they expected.

Coaching time

Paul Pruitt grew up in Memphis, Tennessee, in a loving Christian family. The church tradition in which he was raised placed great emphasis on salvation; every message ended with a call for the hearers to examine their own lives and be sure that they were saved. Unfortunately, there was less emphasis placed on discipleship, or growing in the faith, and so as he grew up Paul took his Christian life somewhat for granted.

Paul had a plan for his life: he wanted to be a professional baseball player, and this ambition drove him through high school. However, like many teenagers, he made a few mistakes and bad choices, and these caused him some problems. He wanted to be sure that he was saved, but he was aware of a deep-seated fear that he was not living his life the way God wanted him to: he just hoped he could get away with doing what he wanted. By the time he was in his senior year in high school, things were going well for him – he succeeded in winning a baseball scholarship to university – but his awareness of the deep conflict in his life made him deeply depressed, to the extent that at one point he almost attempted suicide. He was churning around in a muddle of rebellion, sin and fear, because he no longer had any sense of assurance in God.

He knew that this depressed, anxious self did not match up with the dynamic young baseball player he wanted to be, but he could see no way out of his confused feelings. It was at this low point that something life-changing happened to him. His mother worked in a department store, and Paul would occasionally drive the family car to collect her from work. One evening he was early, and wandered into a nearby bookshop to kill time. He picked up a book called *A Handbook for Christian Athletes*, which was designed like a training manual, except that the focus was on Jesus. It pointed out that if Jesus had been an athlete, he would have been perfect: not in the sense of getting the greatest scores or breaking all the records, but in pleasing God.

It also included a description of the crucifixion, with a medical analysis of what happened to someone who suffered death on the cross. For the first time, Paul saw that suffering as tangible, and realised that Jesus had died for him. When he came to the text in Mark 8:36, "What good is it for a man to gain the whole world, yet forfeit his soul?" he realised what he had been doing – chasing after whatever the world could offer, without any thought for his soul. It was as though he was looking at Jesus on the cross, and saying, "I know what you're doing, but I don't want it right now.

I want to go my own way." The very thought of being able to say that to God filled him with painful remorse and shame. He realised that he had always put himself first, ahead of whatever God wanted for him.

He bought the book, took it home, and finished reading it that night. That was the night when he finally gave his life to God, and felt the joy of knowing that he had truly placed himself in God's hands. He still did not know much about God, however: he expected that the first thing to happen would be that all the good things he had coveted so much – his baseball scholarship, his university career – would be taken away from him. So he was surprised and pleased to find that a month later he was at university in Ohio, taking up his scholarship and settling into an exciting student life, studying and playing sport.

On his first Sunday at church, he met someone who would take his Christian life further: Bill Jones. Bill ran a Bible study course especially for athletes, and invited Paul to join it. There he was discipled for the next three years, growing spiritually and developing a deeper understanding of the Christian life. The Campus Crusade materials they used had a way of asking hard questions: "What are you doing with your life? What really matters to you?" Paul found these questions challenging and uncomfortable, since in his case the answer was usually: "Becoming a famous baseball player."

Over the next two or three years, God worked in Paul to expose his youthful selfishness, and bring him to the point where he was capable of asking himself how much he was willing to give up for God.

In his second year the Bible study course began to talk about mission, and challenge the students to talk to one other person each week about Christ. Paul began to evangelise his teammates, arranging talks and testimonies; he had gone full circle back to the teaching of his childhood church, and asked once again: "Are you sure of your salvation?", but this time in the full understanding of what it means to grow in the Christian life. On his second summer vacation he turned down an opportunity to play summer-league baseball, and chose instead to take part in a beach mission at Myrtle Beach, South Carolina. He found it difficult but satisfying. In his third summer he went on a short overseas mission to the Philippines, showing a film about Jesus and listening to the team of seven Filipinos giving their testimonies. He was drawn to the world of mission, and increasingly questioning his own ambitions.

Back at the university, Paul was less satisfied with the prospect of his planned baseball career. Looking at life in the context of God's kingdom, it was hard to see great significance in hitting a little white ball. The game which had been the focus of all his attention for so long was becoming meaningless. He felt uncomfortable about the hours he spent on the practice field, and at last he made the decision that he would spend the rest of his life doing what God wanted him to. Baseball no longer had the power to fulfil all his longings and his new ambition to be whatever God wanted him to be.

God's timing

During Paul's senior year in college, a friend of his visited Malaysia, and came back full of excitement about missionary work. He wanted to go to China next, and tried to encourage Paul to go with him; he gave him a brochure about work there. Paul thanked him and absent-mindedly filed it among his papers. He had never really thought much about China or its people, and he was busy studying to finish his course.

After college he went home to his family in Memphis. In the absence of any plans for his career, he lived at home and worked in his father's business, though he was praying hard about the future. He wondered whether God wanted him to be involved in mission or ministry, but he had no clear ideas at all.

Then, one night in April 1982, he woke suddenly at about 3 a.m. He was absolutely certain that God spoke to him, saying, "Get out that China brochure." The feeling was so insistent that he got out of bed and began sleepily searching in his desk for the brochure. He scarcely remembered seeing it, some nine months and a house-move ago, and yet he was quite sure that it was God's voice speaking to him, and so he was equally sure that the leaflet must be there somewhere. At last he found it, and discovered that it contained a detailed application form – he filled it in laboriously, while the household slept around him. It was 7.30 a.m. before he finished writing the full testimony it required. When he reached the back page of the form, he found a note in small print: the deadline for applications was that day! At least, he thought, he had finished it in plenty of time. In the US, the postman picks up the outgoing mail from the mailbox at the same time as he delivers the incoming mail, and Paul knew that the postman never came to his house before 10.00 a.m. Nevertheless, he went downstairs at once and dropped the letter in the box. That day, the postman arrived at 8.30 a.m. God's timing was precise.

The result was that Paul spent part of that summer in China, and everything that had been happening fell into place. He knew that he was called to be a missionary, and that he wanted to work among the Chinese people: a few weeks in Beijing were enough to fill him with love for the people he met, and a concern for the millions who had no opportunity to hear the gospel.

He knew, however, that he needed training for this task, and so the following year he enrolled at the Columbia Graduate School of Bible and Mission (now called Columbia International University). There, he gained the theological training he needed, and also met his future wife.

Paul's flatmate was Japanese, and one day he pointed out Naomi, a lovely Japanese girl: "She wants to go to China, too," he said. Paul and Naomi quickly realised how closely their plans and ideals matched, but their parents were less than enthusiastic. Although they were not opposed to the relationship in principle, they knew how difficult a mixed marriage could be. They were concerned about any mixed-race children the couple might have, as well as the impact on their ministry. Paul and Naomi put their relationship on hold for 18 months while they finished their studies. Then, to their surprise, they suddenly found that there were no obstacles in their way. Both sets of parents changed their minds and supported them, and in 1986 they were married.

First base: Taiwan

Even though Paul knew in 1982 that he wanted to work among the Chinese, it was ten years before that dream became a reality.

After their marriage, both the Pruitts settled into jobs, Paul working in an architectural firm, and Naomi teaching in primary school. During this time, they applied for missionary work and were accepted by OMF, and in 1988 Paul left his job and went to work in an OMF regional office; their first child, Joshua, was born in November 1988. Everything was on track for their departure to the East in March 1989.

However, their plans were held up by the growing unrest in China: students there had gone on strike to demand dialogue with the government on democratic reform. Protesters were filling the streets of Beijing daily, in spite of the imposition of a curfew, and it became clear that the government would have to take decisive action. These events culminated in the massacre of protesters in Tiananmen Square on 4th June, but long before then the mission authorities had seen that – with the current political sensitivities and enhanced government caution – it was not a good time for foreign nationals to enter the country. Paul and Naomi, with their young baby, were diverted to Japan, where they occupied themselves in raising support among Naomi's church friends there. By July, it was clear that entry into China was not an option, and so when they completed their orientation course in Singapore they chose to work in Taiwan.

They had intended this to be a short placement, but in the end they stayed for two and a half years; they were learning Mandarin Chinese with an excellent supervisor, and gathering all the religious vocabulary which was so important to them. Paul taught an English Bible course in their local church in Taichung, and they shared in some pastoral work. In March 1991, their daughter Hosanna was born, so Naomi was kept busy caring for two small children.

Eventually their longed-for placement came through: Paul would be able to work in China as an English teacher. This meant gaining the teaching expertise and the qualifications which would be acceptable to the Chinese government, and so the family moved to Hong Kong, where Paul undertook four months' training in teaching English as a foreign language. It was September 1992 before they finally moved to the town of Lanzhou, in Gansu Province, to begin their work in China.

Second base: China

Lanzhou is a relatively large city of around 2 million people; a third of the population is Hui Muslim. At that time, however, it was not as sophisticated a place as Beijing or Shanghai, and living conditions were extremely simple. Paul and Naomi lived in the university, but even there the water supply was limited, and hot water had to be collected from a distant part of the campus and carried home to give the children rather tepid baths. Lanzhou is a dry and dusty place on the edge of the Gobi Desert: sandstorms could blow up in minutes, and were dangerously powerful. When the wind blew in off the desert (called "yellow sands" in Chinese) everyone scrambled to get inside as quickly as possible.

Naomi cared for the children and the home,

and spent some time with non-Christian Chinese women she met in the town; she also had some ministry with a few local Chinese believers. She welcomed the students into their home as much as was permissible: foreigners still had to take care that they did not offend the authorities.

Paul taught in two schools: the Gansu Education College, and the North-West Minority Institute. In the Minority Institute some 96 per cent of the students were Chinese Muslims, with some Tibetans. Like many missionaries in "closed" countries, Paul was employed primarily as a professional, with his missionary role a secondary one. However, his teaching workload was heavy, and he found this increasingly frustrating. He had no time for any of the evangelism he longed to do; he struggled to keep up with preparing classes and marking assignments.

On its own, this would not have been too great a problem, and he would have soldiered on, hoping that things might improve. However, there were also family difficulties: Joshua was ready to start school, but there was no suitable school anywhere nearby. They had tried the local Chinese kindergarten, but he had been unhappy there. Memories of the war were still strong in China, even after forty years, and when the children knew that Joshua was Japanese they would tease him and imitate machine-guns firing at him. He spoke both English and Japanese, but very little Chinese, and the teacher felt that dealing with the needs of a foreign child took up too much of her time. In any case, Naomi had little confidence in the teaching methods employed in the local schools, and was wondering whether they would have to send Joshua to boarding-school, an option none of them wanted.

Then they heard that Naomi's father was ill: a heart condition was diagnosed. She was anxious to visit him, and the grandparents wanted to see their grandchildren. Just when they were considering making a visit to Japan, they heard of a missionary need which spoke to their hearts. A Taiwanese couple had started a Chinese church in Tokyo, and desperately needed help. It was a task that both Paul and Naomi felt called to. They could continue their work with the Chinese people they loved, and use their language skills, but Paul would be relieved of the professional teaching burden which was hampering his missionary work. In addition, there would be schooling available for their children, and they would be near to Naomi's family if there was a crisis in her father's health. All the signs were pointing to a move to Japan, and they applied to OMF for a transfer.

Meanwhile, they paid a visit to the USA, where their third child, Justin, was born in Paul's home town of Memphis. The change of location was agreed, and they set off back to the OMF language school in Hokkaido, where Paul (the only non-Japanese speaker in the family) had to start on the uphill struggle to master yet another non-European language.

Third base: Japan

Their work in Tokyo was a mixture of church planting and pastoral work. The congregation was an interesting one, consisting mainly of Chinese-speaking war orphans. During the war, Japan had invaded and occupied China, and many Japanese had settled and begun to raise families there. When the Red Army advanced across the country to reclaim it for the Communists, the Japanese fled for their lives, sometimes leaving their children behind. Many of these children were cared for by Chinese families, so they grew up within that culture, speaking only Chinese. In the 1980s the Japanese government invited these children, now grown up, to return to Japan, the country of their birth. It was an invitation which was enthusiastically taken up, for living in Japan was an attractive prospect, especially for relatively poor Chinese from the rural north-east regions of China. Many of them were now trying to settle down in Japan, find jobs, and often locate their birth parents, but of course they had forgotten any Japanese they ever knew, and were effectively, in terms of culture and language, Chinese immigrants.

This time a great deal of the work fell upon Naomi. She was a native Japanese speaker, and while Paul had done well in mastering the basics of the language so that he could converse with people, his fluency did not approach Naomi's.

She was the one that people turned to when they wanted a letter translated and explained to them, or help with job applications. One man had come to Japan with his wife and children, hoping to contact his mother. He had found her, but she spoke no Chinese and he spoke little Japanese; they needed Naomi to make telephone calls and arrangements, and to translate for them when they met. With three children at home, and pregnant with a fourth, this time it was Naomi who was overburdened with work. When Jeremy was born in 1997 it seemed that some change would have to happen; it was simply too hard for her to carry such a large proportion of the pastoral care. Meanwhile, although Paul was leading the church worship and preaching, he felt unable to contribute to the pastoral work – often he would stay at home to look after the children while Naomi was out visiting. The see-saw of their shared missionary work had tilted the other way, and he felt that their little congregation began to judge him negatively.

After four years, they were once again unhappy about the balance of their work. Paul felt particularly responsible, as though it was always he who was finding problems in their situation. In China, he had felt too constrained by the demands of his teaching role, and unable to work properly as a missionary. Now he had more time and freedom for pastoral work, but was hindered by trying to work in Japanese as well as Chinese – two languages that were new to him. He wondered whether he was simply making difficulties for himself, and whether he should leave missionary work altogether. Perhaps he should take a secular job, teaching English as a foreign language in Japan, for instance, and resign himself to the level of evangelism that could be expected of any Christian who had a full-time job.

He prayed hard about this, questioning everything and looking back over the milestones of his Christian life to see whether he had been deceiving himself about the signs he had acknowledged as coming from God. Somehow, he couldn't believe that he had been wrong about his calling to mission, but the fact remained that he did not feel that his work was as fruitful as it should be, and he did not yet feel that he was in the place where God wanted him to be.

Then, in 1998, he went to Hong Kong to attend a Diaspora conference, and there he met Keith Ranger, an OMF missionary with twenty-nine years' experience. Keith talked with enthusiasm about the opportunities and needs in the Chinese church worldwide: he explained that in the USA the provision for Chinese Christians was well-staffed and well-resourced; in the UK, however, the church was poor by comparison, and there was a great need for Chinese-speaking Christians to lead evangelism. Once again, Paul felt that familiar tug of the Spirit: here was a need that they were eminently well qualified to meet.

Back in Japan, he shared his thoughts and prayers with Naomi. Long email conversations with Keith clarified some of the issues, and more and more they began to feel that England could be the right place for them. It would enable them to work with Chinese people, using their skills in the Chinese language, but without the added difficulty for Paul of working in a country where a third language was spoken. This time, of course, it would be Naomi who was working in her third language, but she had been fluent in English for so long that this was not such a problem for her as working in his newly acquired Japanese had been for Paul.

In 1999 the family made yet another move, to the UK, with responsibility for work with Chinese in the whole of the south of England.

Home plate: England

When they arrived in Oxford, Paul and Naomi had no one to guide them in their work – it was entirely new ground. Neither of them had ever been to the UK before, and they found that in spite of their ease in an English-speaking country, there were still culture shocks. Like many other foreigners, they were unprepared for the discovery that such a small percentage of the population is churchgoing or Christian. They had expected a country with such a long Christian history and heritage to have more believers, and a greater Christian influence in society. There seemed to be less support for mission than they had imagined.

Their first task was to locate the Chinese students who were their primary target population, so they started out by contacting organisations who were working with international students in any context, and trying to meet Chinese students. Once they had a few contacts – who were always delighted to meet people in England who could speak Chinese – they began a low-key networking operation, inviting students to bring their friends for meals, getting to know them and offering them a chance to make friends and share their experiences and concerns.

The breakthrough came after eighteen months of patient befriending. In the summer of 2001, they arranged a two-day meeting, and invited a Chinese scholar, Leaf Huang, as guest speaker. Leaf Huang is a gifted genetic scientist from the University of Pittsburg, and he speaks on topics of interest to the new generation of Chinese students, such as the role of materialism in society and the challenges of science and religion. He also works with a gifted worship leader, and his wife leads seminars on marriage topics. The meeting was a huge success: over 100 students came on the first evening, and after the second day 35 Chinese indicated that they had accepted Christ as Lord of their lives, or that they wanted to know more.

After this, Paul and Naomi recognised the need to follow up all these expressions of interest, so they set about organising a series of Bible studies. Several events combined to make this possible. They had originally planned to visit the US that summer for Paul's parents' 50th wedding anniversary, but somehow their visas were lost and they were unable to travel; they were sad to miss the celebrations, but it left them free to make all the arrangements and begin planning the studies. Then they were offered a new house with a large, bright conservatory room at the back overlooking the garden: ideal for holding large house-groups. They moved at the end of August, and were ready to begin the studies in September.

There were two separate groups: one for Christians (with six or seven regular members), and the other for "Seekers" (with around twelve members), although often the Christians brought along their non-Christian friends with them.

Contact with other churches where there were groups of Chinese students revealed a huge demand for Bible study materials, especially in a bilingual format. Often, the leaders would be English people with no Chinese language, but their students might be newly arrived in this country, with little English. They would quickly become discouraged if they found the materials too hard for them to follow, so each study needed to be written in Chinese, too. Paul at once set about producing these bilingual Bible studies. One is a six- to eight-week apologetics course, covering the historicity of Jesus, the reliability of the Bible (including biblical archaeology), evolution, the evidence for design, and the claims of Jesus (as liar, lunatic or Lord); the second covers the Gospel of John for seekers; the third is a survey of the Old Testament for new believers.

A typical request came from a pastor at the University of Hertfordshire. He had encountered many Chinese students at the University; how could Paul help him to reach out to them? This has now become an enabling role for Paul and Naomi. Not only can they put the study materials into willing English hands, but they can also provide the training which will give the leaders an insight into the Chinese culture and mindset, showing them the best ways of explaining the gospel.

Initially, Paul was preaching in both English and Chinese churches, but he is now so busy locally that there is little opportunity to travel. The next step is to host a series of evening meetings on the subject of science and faith at the beginning of the academic year for new Chinese arrivals; he estimates that they can draw between 100 and 200 people to each meeting.

They are also collecting a library of Chinese books to loan to their students, and building up a base of trained and well-informed Chinese Christians, who can help them reach out to the places where groups of Chinese have gathered.

A vision for the future

Paul and Naomi have a vision for their work in the UK. They know that many of their Chinese students come to Oxford for two years on language courses; they then disperse to other

English cities to take up courses at universities and colleges. The vision is for a network of contacts across the UK, so that wherever the students go, they can be put in touch with a group of Chinese Christians who can support and nurture them in their faith. With easy contact by email, and many Christian students already moving on, this is on its way to becoming a reality. They see several hundred international students coming to Christ each year in Oxford alone, with around 50 of them being Chinese contacts of theirs.

There is a mission field among the Chinese in the UK, and it is ripe for harvest. Of all the international ministries, the Chinese is the most responsive: the annual Easter conference for Mandarin-speakers at Cliff College in Sheffield is four years old now; it regularly attracts 400 people. There are around 4,000 Chinese in Oxford alone, and they are hungry to know about God: they go eagerly to meetings and Bible studies.

Paul is keen to deliver a wake-up call to the UK. He points out that it is hard to start a discussion with your English neighbours about Christ; they will probably be embarrassed and avoid you for weeks! Strangers may well shut the door in your face if you start calling on them to talk about the gospel. But the Chinese are not offended: they are interested and intrigued and want to know more. They think it is quite natural for you to talk, on a first meeting, about something so important to you.

The richest field for mission in the UK is among the international visitors here, and for the Chinese it is a God-given opportunity to hear the gospel. We need the wisdom to recognise this and the courage to share in the work.

Looking back

Paul hesitates when he speaks about the many different places where he and Naomi have served. He wonders whether it shows a lack of "stickability", a tendency to move on whenever things were hard. Yet he admits that he wouldn't have missed any part of it – and he can see what each stage of their journey added to their experience.

In Taiwan, they developed their excellent Chinese language skills, something that enabled them to master different dialects when it was needed, and have the comprehensive religious vocabulary required for writing teaching materials and Bible studies.

Their years in rural China developed their understanding of the Chinese, and gave them the credibility they needed when meeting Chinese elsewhere in the world: here were people who had taken the trouble to live and work in China in their eagerness to reach the Chinese people with the gospel.

Their time in Japan gave them experience in pastoral work and a deeper understanding of the Chinese mind-set. It also taught them a great deal about themselves, and helped them to evaluate their missionary skills, and see how they could be most useful.

Paul and Naomi's journey took them in directions they never imagined, and brought them to an exciting and fruitful mission in a place they least expected to find it. They never chose the easy route, but listened in trust to the promptings of the Holy Spirit when he indicated that it was time to move on. Their story shows that God's preparation is thorough, and he knows exactly what is needed to equip his servants for the tasks he has in mind for them. God wanted Paul and Naomi in this unusual ministry, and took them the long way round – via Taiwan, China and Japan – to find their mission field in England.

Refined in
the Fire

Dave drifted slowly back to consciousness. Where was he? Opening his eyes was too much effort. He shifted uncomfortably in the bed, and suddenly became aware of searing pain. His arms, his chest, his face – they were all burning. What had happened to him? Burning – that was it. He recalled a flash, a sheet of flame, the children screaming. Why couldn't he remember any more? Everything hurt so much.

He groaned and opened his swollen eyelids. There beside the bed was his wife, Bev, biting her lip with anxiety. He couldn't speak. A nurse came and held an invalid cup to his lips, and he managed to sip a little of the cool liquid, before slipping back into a drowsy haze.

Walking. He could remember walking, on and on, with someone beside him. And there had been a truck, jolting along the potholed road, when every bump had sent more pain shooting through his throbbing head. He hadn't been able to feel his arms and hands, then; they had been numb and white – he remembered looking at them as if they belonged to someone else. Then they came to the hospital, and the doctors. He had tried to tell them what was wrong, but somehow his lips wouldn't make the words, and he couldn't seem to speak the language any more.

They had peeled off his burned skin and covered him in ointment and bandages. That was when the pain had started. He tried to tell them that wasn't how you treated burns any more, but they didn't understand. Just kept on torturing him. And through it all he had kept praying. When he could think of nothing else but the pain, when he kept slipping in and out of consciousness, when he couldn't speak aloud, except to cry out in agony, he kept praying: "Lord Jesus, please help me. Watch over Bev and the children. Oh, Lord Jesus, help me."

He opened his eyes again. There, at the foot of the bed, was a strange figure: a slim brown tribesman with spiky, black hair, wearing a ragged shirt and trousers – Mariano Lakoy. It was

Mariano who had walked beside him on that endless, painful road. It was Mariano who had helped him onto the bed and spoken to the doctors for him, who had prayed for him and stayed with him. Dave made a huge effort to move his parched lips.

"Mariano," he whispered. "Thank you."

Of all nations

The island of Mindoro lies south of Manila in the Philippines. Jagged mountain ranges form the spine of the island, which is edged with palm-fringed beaches and busy coastal towns. In between lie dense green forests of ebony, mahogany, bamboo and lush ferns, hiding deep valleys and wide rivers. It was visited by Chinese traders in the thirteenth century, annexed by the Spanish in the sixteenth century and by the Americans in the nineteenth century. Filipino people have long lived in the lowland areas, farming and logging and building up trading ports and small towns.

However, the earliest inhabitants were the Mangyan tribespeople, who retreated into the mountains from all these immigrants, continuing to live their traditional way of life, practising slash-and-burn farming, clearing small areas of jungle to grow yams and maize, and building their houses on bamboo stilts. In the 1950s, when the first OMF missionaries came to Mindoro, an anthropologist estimated that there were some 15,000 Mangyan living an iron-age existence in the upland valleys – there later proved to be about three times that number.

Why should anyone disturb this peace-loving, simple people? Their way of life had been largely unchanged for centuries; the forest provided them with bananas, coconuts, wild pigs and deer for food, clean rivers for water, and palm and bamboo for building shelters. Yet their life was not idyllic. Whole villages would move inland to avoid the encroaching civilisation of the lowlanders, who would force the gentle Mangyan to work in the mahogany forests for little or no pay, and beat them if they refused. Often, they were driven from the jungle land they had cleared with their own hands, as the lowland people expanded their own farms. Uneducated and illiterate, they had no voice in the government, which sent policemen to force their young people to leave their villages and live in government schools in the towns. With no access to doctors or medicines, they were prey to infections, and many of their children died in infancy.

Worse, however, was the oppressive regime of their native religion. The Mangyan were animists: they believed that their every action was observed by spirits living in the rocks, trees and rivers. If the spirits approved of you, all would go well; if not, misfortune followed you – accidents, crop failures, illness, death. The Mangyan lived in superstitious fear, constantly looking for signs to tell them what to do. If they stumbled over a tree root when setting out on a journey, they would turn back – the spirits disapproved. If the koykolo bird called in the morning, there would be trouble that day. If someone had a bad dream, the spirits were telling him to abandon whatever he was planning – to plant a field, or build a house, or choose a wife. They were hampered at every turn by what the spirits wanted – or by what their shaman told them they must do. Illness could only be cured by appeasing the spirits with sacrifices, so many Mangyan sank further and further into poverty and hunger as they sacrificed their last chicken or pig in a vain attempt to regain their health.

There were six main tribal groups of Mangyan living in the hidden upland villages of Mindoro: the Iraya and Alangan in the north-west of the island, the Tadyawan and Tawbuid of the central region, and the Buhid and Hanunoo of the south. All spoke unwritten languages as well as some Tagalog, the general Filipino language, which was useful for trading purposes. The only way for the missionaries to begin to communicate directly was to find Filipinos who knew Mangyan living in the fringe areas, who could begin to translate and help them with their language study. Most of the missionaries used wind-up record players and recordings of gospel readings made in the Mangyan languages. They would play these to any tribespeople they met as a way of explaining why they had come – and then they would begin to teach in Tagalog and learn the local language.

Making contact

This was the world into which Dave and Bev Fuller stepped when they went to work on Mindoro Island. Both were OMF missionaries, who had met and married in Manila. Both were filled with a desire to reach these primitive, fear-filled people, to free them from their enslavement to the spirits which ruled their lives, and to tell them the good news that there was a greater spirit than these: a God who loved them and gave his life for them. Dave was a Canadian; his father was a Methodist minister who travelled around in his ministry to shanty men and lumber workers. Bev was an American who had already made history of a sort: together with Morven Brown she had become one of the first people to make real contact with the Alangan people of north-west Mindoro. Some missionaries had seen some of the men in the forest; so had some of the lumber workers who travelled through the territory looking for mahogany trees, and so had the government workers who occasionally sprayed for mosquitoes in an effort to reduce the incidence of malaria. No one had ever seen the women and children, though, and they simply assumed that this tribe had very few womenfolk.

Bev and Morven had been guided by some Filipino friends to a remote valley where they met some Alangan men, who were amazed to hear the women speak to them in their own language. Their leader was called Presidente, and Bev asked if they might accompany him to the main village and speak to the rest of his people. To their delight, he agreed, and led them through the jungle to the clearing where the rest of the people lived. The men constructed a shelter above the huts where the tribe lived during the hot, dry season, and Bev and Morven were invited to stay there. They played their Alangan language records and spoke to the people about the God who loved them, and about Jesus, who understood them because he had lived on earth as a man. They had the full attention of all the village leaders, who sat and listened hungrily all evening. As they lay down to sleep that night, they knew they had taken the first steps toward reaching these shy and secretive people.

The next day they looked out to see, for the

first time, the everyday life of an Alangan village. Toddlers played in the dirt alongside the village animals – pigs, chickens and dogs; older children carried bamboo tubes of water from the river for drinking and cooking, and women were tending the fires and preparing breakfast. They shared their food with the missionaries – it turned out to be rice and boiled bat! The two women knew that they had been granted a rare privilege: because they spoke the people's language, they were able to communicate with them directly, and because they were women, the women and children of the tribe did not hide from them, as they had hidden from the male missionaries and others who had passed nearby before.

Bev and Morven were able to return to the village some three months later, by which time they had made another plan. What if they were to walk across the whole island of Mindoro, from west to east, contacting as many Alangan as they could find? When they told Presidente, he arranged guides to take them from village to village, leading them to the hidden places in the hills where no white people had ever travelled.

They walked for eight days, and in each village they were welcomed, and people listened eagerly to the good news they told them. Bev and Morven knew that it would take much more teaching to help the people to learn the power of the love of Jesus, and to encourage them to give up their habitual fear of the spirits, but everywhere they went they were asked to return. The people were eager to hear about a new way of life, in which they did not have to be ruled by fear, and they wanted to know the God who loved them and cared for them.

Teach us his ways

Shortly after their marriage, Bev and Dave attended the first Inter-tribal Believers' Conference on Mindoro. The dozen or so missionaries who had been working on the island for the last six years were seeing the first fruits of their work: the tiny churches all across the island had sent delegates to worship together and discuss their needs. They sang hymns in Tagalog, their common language, and took it in turns to lead the prayer and teaching. Dave was overwhelmed with the magnitude of what was happening. Not long ago, these people had cowered in their mountain retreats, afraid to meet people from outside their area, and controlled by the whims of evil spirits. Now they were travelling across their land to meet other tribes and share what they knew about God's love. "This is what it will be like in heaven," thought Dave, "everyone worshipping together, with culture, race, education, ability, all forgotten and unimportant beside the wonder of praising God."

One idea had emerged strongly from all their discussions. What the tribal leaders wanted most of all was to learn more – about following Jesus, about the Bible, about how to lead their churches, and how to reach other people with the good news. How could they learn all these things, scattered as they were in their tiny mountain communities? There were only a handful of missionaries to teach them, in an island of 6,000 square miles, and there were hundreds of villages still unreached.

The solution was to run short-term Bible schools. The missionaries could come to a central village for three weeks or so, and a group of tribal leaders could gather there to study, and then go back and pass on what they had learned. Dave was amazed at their insistence, and their willingness to give up their time in this way. It was no small sacrifice for people as poor as this to take time out from tending their fields and their animals to stay at a Bible school.

Over the next four years the Bible schools were established. The Mangyan were accustomed to moving around, shifting their villages according to the season and building their flimsy bamboo shelters close to their fields or deep in the jungle. It was not hard to build an extra shelter or two for the visitors, or let them sleep in a "big-house" with other members of the tribe. The new believers were enthusiastic, and every school was well attended. Moving from place to place meant that no one had to travel very far. Whenever the school was based in their village of Ayan Bekeg, on the slopes of Mount Halcon, Dave and Bev would lead classes and worship sessions for the students.

However, even this could not satisfy the

appetite of the Mangyan for God's word. One by one, people began to approach the missionaries to tell them that they knew they needed their own full-time leaders. Only they knew their people's ways and their hearts well enough to reach them with an understanding of what it meant to be a Mangyan and a believer. They needed missionaries from among their own people.

This was music to Dave's ears! All OMF missionaries knew that their primary aim was to work themselves out of a job — to establish a native church which was self-supporting. They prayed constantly that God would raise up leaders from among the people, with the wisdom and thirst for God's word which would enable them to teach and guide their own church communities. Too often the faith was seen as something "belonging" to the Westerners, in which they alone were the experts. Yet equipping these primitive people with the tools for understanding meant much more than simply telling them Bible stories and teaching them hymns; they needed to be able to read the Bible for themselves, which meant a whole new educational burden for literacy in Tagalog, and obtaining Filipino Bibles. That required more than a three-week stay in the travelling Bible school. It was clear that they needed a bigger, more permanent school where students could attend for three months or so.

A family of believers

Once again, the Mangyan were ahead of the missionaries in developing a new idea. The villagers at Ayan Bekeg volunteered their village as the site for the first session of the main Bible school. They made plans to build a schoolhouse with a split-log floor and a palm-thatched roof, and a house for Frances Williamson, the OMF missionary who would help Dave and Bev with the teaching. They planted extra sweet potatoes wherever they could find space, to provide food for the extra mouths. Messengers came from the other villages who wanted to send students to train; they would support their own delegates. Other believers would look after their crops at home. Those who earned a little cash by working in the lowlanders' fields, or by selling rattan or bananas, would contribute money to buy

Bibles and notebooks. As brothers in Christ, they would share what they had, to gain what they wanted: new life in Christ, with pastors of their own to lead and teach the churches.

It was an exciting time for Dave and Bev. In the first term there were four typhoons in two weeks, and everyone worked hard to repair the schoolhouse when the bamboo walls blew down. The Tawbuid and Tadyawan had never been so far away from their homelands, and the Buhid from the south were not used to the cold, wet weather. Yet there was a cheerful determination about the men who sat in the schoolroom each morning, or worked in the fields in the afternoons, or struggled to learn to read Tagalog in the evenings. They had a common purpose, and they sang their hymns and prayed with their Christian brothers and sisters from other tribes.

Dave had only one concern: keen as they were to learn, many of the Mangyan still looked up to their missionary teachers as the experts. It was hard for them to see that they were all equal in God's family. As brothers and sisters in Christ, the power of the Holy Spirit was available to everyone, Mangyan tribesman or Canadian missionary, but this was a difficult lesson for them to learn. After all, the Western teachers seemed to have everything: they could read, speak several languages, write letters, prescribe medicines, communicate with the government. Surely they were more important in God's family than the lowly tribesman? Dave found it hard to counter this unspoken assumption.

A steadfast spirit

Meanwhile, Bev and Dave had settled into their own family routine. They both taught for three months at a time in the Bible school, though Bev had her hands full with their growing family: six-year-old Jon, four-year-old Esther, and two-year-old David.

Jon was home from his first year at school in Malaysia, and happy to meet up with his Alangan friends in the village. All three spoke fluent Alangan – perhaps better than their parents – and were healthy and happy. They didn't seem to have suffered at all from growing up in a bamboo shack and playing in the dirt with the village pigs and chickens. Bev looked at Esther as she reached out for a cockroach scuttling by her foot. Sometimes the thatched ceilings were crawling with cockroaches, and Bev had become almost used to them. When an infestation got too bad, the Mangyan simply moved out of a house, burned it to the ground and built another. It was a very effective means of pest control! Bev was amazed at how relaxed she had become about raising a family in these conditions.

She checked on the bread she was cooking. Mostly, they ate rice and sweet potatoes, but it was good to have some "home cooking" sometimes, for a treat. Baking was a challenge, though. They had a small metal oven which could be placed on top of a kerosene pressure stove; it got just hot enough to bake a loaf. The stove had to stand in an empty five-gallon tin, to protect it from the draughts which whistled through the grass walls of the house. The flame could so easily be blown out by the wind.

It was while she was checking the bread that she noticed a small flame around the pump of the stove, and called Dave to look.

"Something's wrong," he said. "I'll just carry it outside for safety." A tiny hole in the tank had leaked fuel into the bottom of the tin. When he picked it up, the flames connected with the hot fuel and the whole stove exploded into a ball of fire. The children screamed, and Dave dropped the stove on the floor and pushed the children out of the door to safety. Trapped in the house behind the stove, Bev climbed out of the window and tumbled to the ground, just as the whole house was engulfed in flames. She stood looking at it for a moment. Everything they owned was in there – all their clothes, their books, their teaching notes and their Bibles.

She made her way round to the front of the house, and found that things were far worse than she had thought. Dave was badly burned; the skin on his face and arms was turning white. He was looking confusedly at his hands. "What should I do?" he asked her.

"Run to the river and get in the water," said Bev, "perhaps it will cool the burns."

Mangyan friends were running up now,

soothing and holding the screaming children as Bev helped Dave down the slope to the river.

"Lord, show us what to do," she prayed. "We're eight miles from the nearest road. How can we get help?"

Dave dipped himself in the cool water, and then climbed out. His voice was firm.

"I'll have to start walking straight away," he said. "If I don't, I may not be able to make it. I may go into shock. You stay with the children."

Bev was torn. The children were terrified – even with their Mangyan neighbours to look after them, they needed her to be with them. But how could she let Dave go off alone? He might collapse and die on the road with no one to help him.

Just then Mariano Lakoy, one of the first believers in the village, ran up to them. "I'll go with Dave. Don't worry," he said. Bev watched them set off down the mountain track. They had three miles to walk downhill before they reached the plain, and then another five miles to the road. At midday on one of the hottest days of the year, it was a stiff walk for a fit man, let alone one who was burned and in excruciating pain.

The two men hurried down the mountain as fast as they could go. Dave's skin was blistering, and the hot sun made the pain worse. He kept stumbling over roots and stones on the rough track, and halfway down he stopped.

"Mariano, I'm not sure I can make it. I have to rest."

Mariano held on to him. "You have to keep going, Dave. Sit there, we must pray." He bowed his head. "Our Father," he said, "Dave needs your help. Give him strength to keep him going and protect him from the sun. Help us make it to the road and find a way to get to town. Amen."

They set off again, crossing a rickety bridge over a ravine. At the foot of the mountain they found another river, and Dave was able to bathe again. Then they started the long walk across the plain to the road. Dave was conscious only of plodding on, step after painful step, over and over again. At least the sun didn't seem so hot now – or was he imagining it?

When they finally reached the road, they stopped and looked back westwards. Clouds hung over the path they had taken across the flat land. To the south, it was already raining – and rain would have made the deeply rutted loggers' trail treacherous with slippery mud. To the north, the sun still shone brightly – and if they had been in the sun, Dave's pain would have been agonising. Only the strip of cloud between the two had protected him.

Just then a truck drew up, and gave the two men a lift to the hospital in Calapan.

By now, it was raining in Ayan Bekeg. Neighbours had helped Bev to put out the fire and search the ashes for anything that could be salvaged. When they saw that nothing was left, they brought gifts of food, cooking pots, even money, to begin to replace their losses. They fed and comforted the children, and then Bev and three Mangyan friends gathered some food and drink and set off with the children to follow Dave and Mariano. They slithered down the muddy hillside and walked for hours before catching a bus into the town. The Mangyan, as second-class citizens, were relegated to the back cargo area of the bus, and Bev was proud to sit with them there. How she appreciated their quiet, steadfast loyalty. Jon was wet and shivering with cold and fear, and Mariano's son put his jacket around him.

These were the people who once would never have set foot in a town. Now they fearlessly came with her to the mission house and the hospital, supporting her with their love. God had given the Mangyan a new sense of dignity and worth. She was relieved to see Dave in the hospital, in great pain but safe at last. She had no words to express her thanks to Mariano, who had cared for him all that day.

The prayer of faith

Some months later, Dave had recovered sufficiently to return to Ayan Bekeg with his family. They found a new house already built and waiting for them, and stocked with whatever goods the Mangyan had been able to gather for them. It was a warm welcome, and they appreciated anew how dear these people had become to their hearts. That evening they sat with some of their friends, talking over the past weeks, and telling them how much they had valued and depended on their support and prayers.

"I was so thankful that Dave got to the hospital in time," said Bev, and Dave told them about the unexpected cloud cover which had protected him on his long walk across the plains.

"Isn't it wonderful what God does when you missionaries pray to him?" said one of the Mangyan.

"Wait a minute," said Dave. "It was Mariano who prayed for me – not me!" He showed them James 5:16 in his Bible: "The prayer of a righteous man is powerful and effective." There was a moment's pause, and then Dave saw realisation dawning on every face. God had answered the prayer of a Mangyan for a missionary. They were part of the unfolding of God's care that day – part of the body of Christ, with equal roles to play. When they prayed in faith, their prayers were heard, too: they were all brothers and sisters in Christ.

As Dave said later, "If they understand a little more about their value and importance to God, then it was all worth it.'

ENGLISH-SPEAKING
OMF CENTRES

AUSTRALIA: P.O. Box 849, Epping, NSW 2121
Freecall 1 800 227 154
email: omf-australia@omf.net *www.au.omf.org*

CANADA: 5759 Coopers Avenue, Mississauga ON,
L4Z 1R9
Toll free 1-888-657-8010
email: omfcanada@omf.ca *www.ca.omf.org*

HONG KONG: P.O. Box 70505, Kowloon
Central Post Office, Hong Kong
email: hk@omf.net *www.omf.org.hk*

MALAYSIA: 3A Jalan Nipah, off Jalan Ampang,
55000, Kuala Lumpur
cmail. my@omf.net *www.omf.org*

NEW ZEALAND: P.O. Box 10-159, Auckland
Tel 09-630 5778   email: omfnz@compuserve.com
www.nz.omf.org

PHILIPPINES: 900 Commonwealth Avenue,
Diliman, 1101 Quezon City
email: ph-hc@omf.net *www.omf.org*

SINGAPORE: 2 Cluny Road, Singapore 259570
email: sno@omf.net *www.omf.org*

SOUTHERN AFRICA: P.O. Box 3080,
Pinegowrie, 2123
email: za@omf.net *www.za.omf.org*

UK: Station Approach, Borough Green, Sevenoaks,
Kent, TN15 8BG
Tel: 01732 887299   email: omf@omf.org.uk
www.omf.org.uk

USA: 10 West Dry Creek Circle, Littleton, CO
80120-4413
Toll Free 1-800-422-5330   email: omf@omf.org
www.us.omf.org

OMF International Headquarters:
2 Cluny Road, Singapore 259570